Charles Kingsley

From Death to Life

Fragments of Teaching to a Village Congregation

Charles Kingsley

From Death to Life

Fragments of Teaching to a Village Congregation

ISBN/EAN: 9783337167394

Printed in Europe, USA, Canada, Australia, Japan

Cover: Foto ©Lupo / pixelio.de

More available books at **www.hansebooks.com**

From Death to Life

FRAGMENTS OF TEACHING TO A
VILLAGE CONGREGATION

WITH LETTERS ON THE LIFE AFTER DEATH

BY

CHARLES KINGSLEY

RECTOR OF EVERSLEY

EDITED BY HIS WIFE

London

MACMILLAN AND CO.

AND NEW YORK

1887

All rights reserved.

PREFACE

To general readers the publication of this small volume may seem superfluous, since, during the last few years, the public mind has been saturated with discussions on the great subject of the Life after Death. But to those who have not the leisure or opportunity to consult the valuable and exhaustive works of Dean Plumptre, Professor Birks, Mr. Jukes, and other writers, and who still cling to the teaching of Charles Kingsley, these plain sermons, preached to his own parishioners, and suggestive letters to correspondents—known and unknown—may be both welcome and helpful.

Had his life on earth been prolonged, he

would doubtless have spoken more definitely in public, and so have developed the thoughts, which, before this subject had become an open question, he had had the courage to suggest in all his novels, thereby incurring a charge of heresy in some quarters, while, on the other hand, he opened a door of hope to many a thoughtful, sensitive, and perhaps despairing soul. "*I have much more to say on all this,*" he wrote to a friend many years since, "*only I am not well enough to formulate it, so I must content myself, as I have for some time past, with preaching Christ, . . . sure that if I can show forth to my hearers His light, that of itself will dissipate their darkness.*"

F. E. K.

November 1886.

CONTENTS

	PAGE
I. DEATH	1
II. CHRIST'S DESCENT INTO HELL	15
III. THE REGIONS OF THE DEAD (DIVES AND LAZARUS)	29
IV. COMMEMORATION OF THE BLESSED DEAD	51
V. THE RESURRECTION OF THE BODY	61
VI. THE HOPE OF LIFE	75

APPENDIX

LETTERS ON THE LIFE AFTER DEATH	91
THOUGHTS ON THE ATHANASIAN CREED AND THE INTERMEDIATE STATE	108

Death

"You ask, 'What is the Good?' I suppose God Himself is the Good ; and it is this, in addition to a thousand things, which makes me feel the absolute certainty of a resurrection, and a hope that this, our present life, instead of being an ultimate one, which is to decide our fate for ever, is merely some sort of chrysalis state in which man's faculties are so narrow and cramped, his chances (I speak of the millions, not of units) of knowing the Good so few, that he may have chances hereafter, perhaps continually fresh ones to all eternity."
C. K., *Letters and Memories*, 1852.

". . . My belief is, that God will punish (and has punished already somewhat) every wrong thing I ever did, unless I *repent* —that is, change my behaviour therein ; and that His lightest blow is hard enough to break bone and marrow. But as for saying of any human being whom I ever saw on earth that there is no hope for them ; that even if, under the bitter smart of just punishment, they opened their eyes to their folly, and altered their minds, even then God would not forgive them ; as for saying that, I will not for all the world, and the rulers thereof. I never saw a man in whom there was not some good, and I believe that God sees that good far more clearly, and loves it far more deeply, than I can, because He Himself put it there, and therefore it is reasonable to believe that He will educate and strengthen that good, and chastise and scourge the holder of it till he obeys it, and loves it, and gives up himself to it ; and that the said holder will find such chastisement terrible enough, if he is unruly and stubborn, I doubt not, and so much the better for him. . . ."
C. K., *Letters and Memories*, 1849.

"As long as any other man loves the good and does it, and hates the evil and flees from it, my Catholic Creeds tell me that the Spirit of Jesus, 'the Word,' is teaching that man ; and gives me hope that either here or hereafter, if he be faithful over a few things, he shall be taught much."
C. K., *Letters and Memories*.

SERMON I

Death

EASTER EVEN

"For Christ also hath once suffered for sins, the just for the unjust, that he might bring us to God, being put to death in the flesh, but quickened by the Spirit: by which also he went and preached to the spirits in prison; which sometime were disobedient."—1 PET. iii. 18-20.

HAT is the most sad and fearful thing which puzzles poor human beings like you and me? Is it not Death, and what will become of us after death? And more sad and fearful still—the question, What has become of friends of ours who have died? There are no thoughts so painful and agonising as those which come across us sometimes when we think of their

death, and life after death, and of where they are gone. For how many are there of whom we dare not say "they are gone to heaven," and of whom we have not the heart to say "they are gone to everlasting torment"? When they were alive, we used to love them. And can we be more loving than God, whose very name is Love? So we hope that, in spite of all, God may love them still. When they were alive there was some good in them—much evil and folly, but still some good. We loved them for the good that was in them, and not for the sin and folly. Perhaps God may love them still for that same reason. If any one had said to us, "There is no good in that friend of yours; he is a worthless person. What matter what becomes of him?"—should we not have felt angry and indignant, and answered, "You are unjust. How dare you be so unjust to him? He had his faults, but he is not as bad as you make him out; there is some good in him, if it were but called out. *I* will not hate him, *I* will not despair of him. All the world may cast him off, and trample upon the poor soul, but I will not be so unjust as to turn my back upon him, or give him up utterly as long as I see a spark of good in him." And then when such a man dies we say to ourselves, "I should have been unjust if I had taken no account of the little good there was in him. And God is more just than I, perfectly just. Surely God will take account of the little good that was in him!" And so we cannot make up our minds, or say certainly whether the poor creature who is gone is saved or lost.

And then if we read our Bible, and think solemnly and carefully over what it says, a fresh thought comes over us. If there was some good in him, from whom did that good come? It could come from no one but God. Nothing which comes out of a man's own heart can be good. The imaginations of man's heart are evil continually. If there is any good in any human being, sinner or saint, harlot or apostle, yea, any good in angels or archangels, it must come straight and at first-hand from God, the fountain of goodness; it must be the fruit of God's

Spirit striving with or leading that person's spirit. Bear it in mind, my friends, for it is the doctrine of the Bible, and of the old Fathers who shaped out for us our Creeds, our Litany, our prayers, that all good in every man comes from the Spirit of God, and from Jesus Christ the Word of God, the Light who lighteth every man that cometh into the world.

If it is written, Judge not, that ye be not judged; condemn not, that ye be not condemned, surely we cannot help saying to ourselves:—" This spark of goodness in the poor soul who is gone came from God, for it could have come from no one else. It was a sign that God had not deserted him— that God's Spirit was striving with him to the last—that he had accepted some of the teaching of God's Spirit, though a very little. And how do I know that God has deserted him now that he is dead? How do I know that God's Spirit has left him, and given up teaching him, now that he is dead? Why should I not have some hope for him still?" Ay, why not, my friends? I know not.

The old Romish doctrine of Purgatory, which held that people who are not quite good or quite bad are tormented for their sins—so many years of torment for so much sin—and that their time of punishment can be shortened by others offering masses and saying prayers for them, and so God's just judgment can be escaped by unjust favour,—that doctrine of Purgatory, I say, is, as our Article calls it, "A fond thing vainly invented and grounded on no warranty of Scripture." But the doctrine which too many hold nowadays, that every one who does not go straight to heaven when he dies, goes to everlasting torment, is, I sometimes think, just as "vainly invented" and just as little grounded on any warranty of Scripture, though no one, certainly, will accuse it of being "fond." The only text which even seems to warrant it is one in Ecclesiastes,[1] "Where the tree falleth, there it shall be." But we are men, not trees; and if you will look at the text, you will see that Solomon is not speaking of the next life at all—as he never does

---

[1] Eccles. xi. 3.

in Ecclesiastes—but of giving alms and doing all the good we can before a time of trouble and sorrow comes to us.

Indeed this doctrine seems the more cruel and horrible the more one looks at it; and if it were true, this world would be a miserable place, and the next world more miserable still. For why should God go on sending human beings by millions into the world, if that which our Lord said only of the wickedest of all men, the traitor Judas, is true of five-sixths of them—that it were better for them that they had never been born?

The truth is that the Bible decides nothing on this point; and the Church of England has wisely avoided deciding anything either, and has left us free to hope, as far as the Bible and our own conscience and reason can enlighten us.

I know, for the Bible tells me, that the Lord Jesus died for all mankind, and that therefore He died for the dead as well as for the living. As it is written, "God is not the God of the dead, but of the living."

I know, for my Bible tells me, that if we confess our sins, God is faithful and just to forgive us our sins, and to cleanse us from all unrighteousness; and God is eternal and true and cannot change. And therefore if, after death, any man did repent and confess his sins, God would forgive his sins and cleanse him. I know that after this life every man receives the just rewards or wages of the deeds done in the body, whether they be good or evil; and I know that I, if any man, deserve to go to everlasting torment —I have no doubt about that. Yet I hope that by the merits of my Saviour's blood, I shall not go to torment, but to life everlasting. And yet I am sure and certain from God's Word that I shall receive the just punishment of my deeds, though I trust that I shall not receive the torments which I deserve. And therefore again I can hope for many a man, that though he must receive the just punishment of his deeds, he will not, by the merits of the Blessed Saviour, receive the torment which he deserves. I only hope, I am not sure. I am uncertain enough to be afraid to commit a single sin on the strength of it—uncertain enough to give you all here most solemn warning that for every wilful sin which you commit, the just God who will by no means clear the guilty, will make you and me smart in such a way that we shall wish our right hands were cut off before we had done that sin, and brought on ourselves that bitter punishment—but I am certain enough to preach to you all, for yourselves and for those friends of yours whom you have loved and lost, the words of my text, the blessed words of Easter Eve.

These are hopeful thoughts: but whatsoever they are, they are the thoughts which the Church, I think, intended us to have on Easter Eve. The Gospel for Easter Eve declares to us that our Lord, the Lord Jesus, the Saviour—very Man as well as very God—very God as well as very Man—really and actually died, as you and I shall die—was really and actually buried, as you and I shall be,—really and actually lay in the grave, as you and I shall lie. So He, the new Adam, the Head of all men, tasted death for all men; and therefore He tasted all that comes by death: therefore, as the Creed says, He descended into hell, otherwise His death would not have been a real human death—as it was. And therefore we may believe that He, as the Head of all men, tasted for all men all that can happen to every man after death. Tasted? Yes. But conquered also. He could taste nothing without conquering it, without making it feel that He was its Lord and Master. Therefore our old forefathers used to talk of Christ who "harrowed hell" —that is, broke it up, conquered it and destroyed its power over all who sleep in Him. And therefore the Epistle for Easter Eve[1] is chosen to tell us of those human beings like ourselves — who, though they disobeyed the Lord Jesus while they were living, yet were preached to by Him after they were dead. These were the very people of whom He said, "My Spirit shall not always strive with man." His Spirit strove with them while they were yet on earth: they resisted and disobeyed,

---

[1] 1 Pet. iii. 18-20.

and were drowned by the Flood, and their souls went to some place which the Apostle calls "a prison." Yet even there the Lord, when He died, went and preached to them. St. Peter says expressly that He did not go to punish or terrify them, but to plead with them lovingly and graciously. He says expressly that Christ went and preached to them by the same Spirit by which He was raised from the dead. And we know that that Spirit was the Spirit of God—the Spirit of Righteousness, the Spirit of Love, the Lord and Giver of Life, the Converter, the Sanctifier; the same Spirit which joins the Father and the Son, the Spirit of Love by which the Father so loved the world that He gave His only Son for it; the Spirit of Love, by which the Son so loved the Father that He came to fulfil all His will, even to the death. It was by that same Spirit that Jesus preached to these souls in prison, and therefore you may be sure that His errand was one of mercy and love.

This at least we can say, that if there were some spirits of dead men on whom the

Lord Jesus had mercy after they were dead, perhaps He may have mercy on others. We cannot be sure, but we can hope. We can hope in the mystery of Easter Eve. We can hope in the Lord Jesus, who showed Himself a Saviour and a preacher even while His body lay in the grave. We can find comfort in the thought that wheresoever our dead friends are gone, the Lord Jesus has been there too—that He knows the regions of the dead—that He has passed through them, and broken their gates, and triumphed over them. Therefore we can have hope for many a soul about whom we are anxious and uncertain. We can hope that somehow, and somewhen, and somewhere, the Lord may yet have mercy on them, and grant them repentance unto life, before the last great and awful day comes, when He shall be revealed from heaven in flaming fire, when He shall gather all nations before Him, as a shepherd gathers his flock.

May God grant that we and all we love, and all who love us, and all those even too who do not love us, but may hate us or slander us, and ill-treat us, may find mercy in that day, through the merits of Him who as on this Easter Eve went down into the regions of the dead, and passed through them as a conqueror, triumphing over them openly when He rose on the blessed Easter Morn—and so that through the grave and gate of death we too may pass to our joyful resurrection, not for our own works or deservings, but through the merits alone of Him who liveth and reigneth with the Father and the Holy Ghost one God. For ever and ever. Amen.

Christ's Descent into Hell

May 9, 1855.—" . . . These things are most bitter, and the only comfort which I can see in them is, that they are bringing us all face to face with the realities of human life, as it has been in all ages, and giving us sterner and yet more loving, more human, and more divine thoughts about ourselves, and our business here, and the fate of those who are gone, and awakening us out of the luxurious, frivolous, unreal dream (full nevertheless of harsh judgments, and dealings forth of damnation) in which we have been living so long—to trust in a Living Father who is really and practically governing this world and all worlds, and who willeth that none should perish —and therefore has not forgotten, or suddenly begun to hate or torment, one single poor soul which is past out of this life into some other, on that accursed Crimean soil. All are in our Father's hands; and as David says, 'Though they go down into hell, *He is there.* Oh! blessed thought—more blessed to me at this moment (who think more of the many than of the few) than the other thought, that though they ascend into heaven with your poor lost hero, He is there also. . . ."

C. K., *Letters and Memories*, 1855.

"He fought till he could fight no more, and then died like a hero, with all his wounds in front; and may God have mercy on his soul."

"That last was a Popish prayer, Master Frank," said old Mr. Carey.

"Most worshipful sir, you surely would not wish God *not* to have mercy on his soul?"

"No—Eh? Of course not, for that's all settled by now, for he is dead, poor fellow!"

"And you can't help being a little fond of him still?"

"Eh? Why, I should be a brute if I were not. Fond of him? why, I would sooner have given my forefinger than that he should have gone to the dogs."

"Then, my dear sir, if *you* feel for him still, in spite of all his faults, how do you know that God may not feel for him in spite of all his faults? For my part," said Frank, in his fanciful way, "without believing in that Popish purgatory, I cannot help holding with Plato that such heroical souls, who have wanted but little of true greatness here, are hereafter, by strait discipline, brought to a better mind. . . ."

C. K., *Westward Ho.*

SERMON II

Christ's Descent into Hell

"Fear not; I am the first and the last: I am he that liveth, and was dead; and, behold, I am alive for evermore, Amen; and have the keys of hell and of death."—REV. i. 17, 18.

ONE of the most difficult articles in the whole Apostles' Creed is " He descended into hell," and wise divines, for many hundred years, have differed about the meaning of it. In all the explanations which I have read, I have never found two which agreed exactly with each other. I do not pretend to understand what wiser men do not understand; and therefore the best thing I can do is to tell you what the words meant at first.

What the men who put them into the Creed meant by them—that will be the safest and most honest way.

Now what the Fathers who made our Creeds meant by Christ's descending into hell was this :—

In the first place they believed that they found the doctrine set forth in Scripture.

St. Peter says that David was speaking of Christ when he said, "Thou wilt not leave my soul in hell;" that Christ's soul was not left in hell, but rose again the third day. St. Peter certainly does say that, most plainly.[1] But a thing must be in a place first before it can be left in that place. And therefore when St. Peter says Christ's soul was not *left* in hell, it followed plainly, they said, that His soul must have been in hell some time between His death and resurrection.

And in St. Peter's First Epistle[2] he speaks even more clearly on this matter. He says that Christ went and preached to the spirits (or ghosts) in prison, which some time were disobedient when the long-suffering

---

[1] Acts ii. 31. [2] 1 Pet. iii. 18-21.

of God waited in the days of Noah. And then he goes on to tell us why Christ did so. He says that Christ is really to judge the quick and the dead; and that for that reason the Gospel was preached also to those that are dead, that they might be judged according to men in the flesh; but live according to God in the Spirit. By which he seems to mean that those old sinners received after they died just judgment for their wickedness, but because they had not had the full light of the Gospel to teach them, Christ went and preached to them, to give them, as it were, a fair and full chance of repentance, that they might live according to the Spirit unto God, who willeth that none should perish, but that all should come to the knowledge of the truth. This, I say, seems to be the meaning of St. Peter's words. The Fathers thought that it was the meaning of them. But it is a matter on which no one can speak with authority. Nevertheless God knows, though we do not know. God knows, and God is just.

Now this brings us to another question. Why did our Lord descend into hell?

Some say, nowadays, that He only went down into hell that He might suffer everything which sinners deserved to suffer, and pay all the penalty which mankind had deserved to pay; that as sinners had deserved to die, therefore Christ died; and as sinners deserved to go to hell, therefore Christ went down into hell, that He might bear all for us which we deserved to bear. It may be so, but we do not find it set down expressly in Scripture. And does it not seem safer to keep to what Scripture actually tells us about Christ's descent into hell, as the Fathers did who wrote the Creeds? They, following Scripture, thought that Christ's going down into hell meant a great deal more than some people think that it means. They saw that St. Peter said plainly that Christ preached in hell to the poor souls who were disobedient before the flood; and they honoured Christ enough to be sure that His preaching was not in vain. They were sure that wherever He went, He went about doing good, for God was with Him. Whether He ascended up to heaven, or descended to hell, He carried blessings with Him, for He was *The Blessed One;* and life with Him, for He was *The Life;* and light with Him, for He was *The Light;* and truth with Him, for He was *The Truth;* and salvation with Him, for He was *The Saviour.* And therefore the Fathers believed, as St. Peter says, that Jesus descended into hell that He might deliver the souls of the ancients out of hell.

Now they had had a chance, the Bible says, for Noah had preached to them, and they would not hear him; so they ought to have known better already. And yet our Lord took pity on them, and taught them in the region of the dead. How much more (the Fathers thought) would He teach all those millions of poor heathen who had had no chance of learning what was right, who had died before Christ was born! Surely, they thought, He must have preached to them, and delivered out of that doleful place as many as seemed good to Him.

And the thought made them rejoice in saying:—" I believe that Christ descended into hell, and there led captivity captive; that He descended into the lower parts of the earth, as St. Paul says, that He might spoil principalities and powers—the wicked spirits who had power over men—and triumph over them, making a show of them openly."

For the Fathers delighted to speak of Christ as the Scripture does, as " Him who destroyed death and him that hath the power of death—that is the devil." They delighted to speak of Christ as of Him who *spoiled*, that is, *sacked* and emptied hell. Or, as our old forefathers used to say, Christ that *harrowed hell*,—that is, delivered mankind out of the power of hell, and the devil's usurped and unjust kingdom, and claimed them in baptism for God's children, members of Christ, and inheritors of the kingdom of heaven.

The great divine, St. Augustine, has noble words about this. He says, " Scripture speaks plainly of hell and torments. Then there could be no reason for the Saviour going down into them, but to save poor souls out of those torments." And again, "Wherefore we hold most firmly that Christ died, and was buried, and rose again, and the rest which Scripture tells—among which is this, that He was also in hell, having loosed the powers of hell, by which it was impossible that He could be held; from which pains He is rightly understood to have loosed and freed those whom He chose." "But," he goes on, "whether He freed all the souls which He found there, or only some whom He judged worthy, I cannot yet tell.—We cannot think that Christ went down into hell in vain, to be of no use to those who were shut up there. But who they were it is rash for us to settle." "However," adds the good and wise man, "if we were to say that He set free every soul He found in hell, who would not rejoice if we could prove it to be so?" And the great St. Ambrose goes as far, and says :—"Christ Jesus free among the dead, gave remission to those who were in hell, having loosed the jaws of death." And St. Cyril goes farther still, in a sermon on Easter Eve, and says that, "Christ having utterly spoiled hell, and set open its gates to the souls of those who slept, rose again, leaving the devil alone in his hell."

This is, on the whole, what the Fathers who wrote our Creed meant when they put into it "*He descended into hell.*" This is what they thought the text meant in which our Lord says, "I am He that liveth and was dead, and have the keys of hell and death." More than this I cannot tell you; and after all, more than this we need not know.

We do not know what death is; we cannot know yet what hell is; we cannot know certainly to what sort of place either good people or bad people will go after they die. And it is not necessary for us to know, our Lord tells us. It would do us little good if a ghost were to return from the dead to tell us all that had happened to him in the other world. We fancy that it would. We fancy, as Dives did, that, if one from the dead came back to warn sinners, they would surely repent. But our Lord says positively that it is not so; that if the Jews would not hear Moses and the Prophets, neither would they believe if one rose from the dead.

And so of us. If we will not hear the Bible and the Church, neither should we believe though one rose from the dead.

But one thing we do know. We know Who has been through death and hell. We know Who has conquered death and hell. We know Who has the keys of death and hell, and if He shuts none can open, and if He opens none can shut :—and that is Jesus Christ our Lord. We know now that He is Lord and Master below as well as above. We know now that wherever you go, or I go, or any man goes, when he dies, we can go nowhere but where Christ has been before us; into no place but what He has the keys of, and the power of, and the ordering of, and we may be sure that He will use His power justly, faithfully, lovingly, mercifully. We may trust Him for our own souls, for the souls of our forefathers, for the souls of the poor heathen. For, as some good men have thought, if Christ did deliver out of hell some of the heathen who lived before His time, perhaps He may deliver some who have lived after His time. Who can tell? We cannot be sure; but, as St. Augustine said just now in a like case, "If it were true, who would not rejoice?"

It is no concern of ours, and it need not be, for it is Christ's concern; and if He does it, it will be because it ought to be done.

And meanwhile we may have hope and trust in Him for the souls of all who do not offend of malicious wickedness, or do despite to the Holy Spirit of grace, and to the loving Son, and to the loving Father, Who would have no man to perish, but all to come to the knowledge of the truth. For God hateth nothing that He has made. And if He do *not* hear the everlasting prayer which goes up from the Holy Catholic Church in earth and heaven; if He do not have mercy upon every Jew, Mussulman, heathen, and heretic, who ever was, or will be, on this earth, then it will be *their own* fault, and not the fault of Him, who so loved them that He gave His only-begotten Son—though they, alas! know it not—to die that all mankind might live, and to descend into hell that all mankind might be delivered out of hell.

Therefore fear not. Christ has the keys of death and of hell. He has been through them and is alive for evermore. Christ is the *first;* and was loving and just, and glorious and almighty, before there was any death or any hell. And Christ is the *last;* and will be loving and just, and glorious and almighty as ever, in that great day when all enemies shall be put under His feet, and death shall be destroyed, and death and hell shall be cast into the lake of fire.

To which day may God bring us and all His holy Church safely and speedily; delivering us out of the miseries of a sinful world. May He accomplish the number of His elect and hasten His kingdom; and then whatsoever His kingdom shall be like—for who can tell the glory of it?—this at least we know, that when we wake up after His likeness, we shall be satisfied. Amen.

The Regions of the Dead

"My friend, whosoever you may be who read this, you have very likely heard this parable of our Lord's talked about and preached about often enough; and you have very likely heard things said about it which puzzled and pained you, because they seemed to make God a cruel and unmerciful Being, and to contradict flatly those texts of Scripture which tell us that God is Love, that His Will to man is a Good Will, that His mercy is over all His works, that He is good to the unthankful and the evil, that He so loved the world that He gave His own Son to be the propitiation for the sins of the whole world, that He willeth that none should perish, that His ways are equal—that is, just—and working on one consistent everlasting method, and that when the wicked man turneth away from his wickedness, and doeth that which is lawful and right, he shall save his soul alive. Now if you are at all puzzled in this way, do you not think that the most simple and reasonable plan for you is, to take the parable into your own hands, and, trying to forget what other people say it means, examine for yourself, like a free and rational being, what it really does mean, in its simple, straightforward, literal sense; or, if you have no leisure to do this, to read quietly what I have written here, for the purpose of showing what I think the parable does mean, and what I should have said it meant, if I had found it in any other book, or heard it spoken for the first time? . . ."

C. K., *From unfinished MS.—A Plain Tract for Plain People.*

"Do not rashly count on some sudden radical change happening to you as soon as you die to make you fit for heaven. There is not one word in the Bible to make us suppose that we shall not be in the next world the same persons that we have made ourselves in this world. . . . What we sow here, we shall reap there. It is good for us to know and face this. Any thing is good for us, however unpleasant it may be, which drives us from the only real misery, which is sin and selfishness, to the only true happiness, which is the everlasting life of Christ, a pure, loving, just, generous life of goodness."

C. K., *Good News of God Sermons.*

SERMON III

The Regions of the Dead

DIVES AND LAZARUS

"And it came to pass that the beggar died, and was carried by the angels into Abraham's bosom: the rich man also died, and was buried; and in hell he lift up his eyes being in torments."—LUKE xvi. 22, 23.

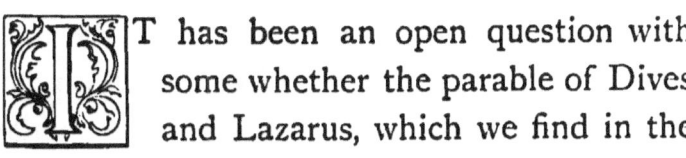T has been an open question with some whether the parable of Dives and Lazarus, which we find in the sixteenth chapter of St. Luke's Gospel, must not be interpreted figuratively throughout. Whether, like many of our Lord's sayings which are popularly supposed to refer to the next life, it does not speak of the fate of the Jewish nation; whether the Scribes and Pharisees (the only men whom our Lord

ever denounced) are not meant by the "rich man" heaped with God's special favour, clothed in purple and fine linen, and faring sumptuously every day; and whether the "poor man" be not the heathens, diseased with sin, fallen to the likeness of brutes, who lay at their doors, longing in vain for teaching.

But there are objections to this interpretation, the most serious of which is, that it would not have been so understood by those who heard it; that they would have naturally supposed our Lord to speak of an actual rich man, an actual poor man, and their actual death and fate. Considering which, it is more safe to interpret the parable, as the first hearers would have done, of two actual men; and reverently and cautiously to look on while our Lord deigns to lift the veil off one nook at least of the world beyond the grave, and to learn what we can from this parable, as He Himself has spoken it, without inserting any doctrines or fancies derived from elsewhere.

And let no one suppose from my interpretation of this parable, that I do not believe that sin is punished, and punished terribly; that we must give an account of the deeds done in the body, whether good or evil; that if a cup of cold water given in Christ's name will in no wise lose its reward hereafter, so shall we answer in the day of judgment for every idle word spoken on earth; and again, that it is better to cut off the right hand or pluck out the right eye than let them lead us into sin.

The subject is especially important just now, when the minds of civilised men are more exercised about the next life and endless punishment therein than they have been for several centuries. Vast numbers, not merely of the most thoughtful and learned, but of the most pious and virtuous, are troubled with honest doubts on the matter. Their numbers are increasing, and it is not too much to say that the fate of the Church of England, and of Christianity itself, in these islands will depend mainly on what decision is arrived at during the next generation or two upon the awful subject of punishment after death. Christianity,

I repeat, will stand or fall therewith and thereby.[1]

How important, therefore, should this parable be to us, for it is almost the only instance in Scripture in which the life after death is certainly described. Many often-quoted texts may not apply to the next life at all; but, I think, this parable *must*. It is an open question, for instance, whether the "outer darkness" spoken of does not mean that outer darkness of barbarism and degradation into which too many nations have sunk back since our Lord's time. It is an open question whether "the worm that dieth not, and the fire which is not quenched" does not refer, like the similar passage in Isaiah, to Gehenna, the Vale of Hinnom, beneath the walls of Jerusalem, where fires were everlastingly kept up to burn the offal of the city, and where the unburied bodies of great criminals were cast out. But is the subject of this parable an open question? *It* surely speaks of the next life. "The

---

[1] *Vide* "The Shaking of the Heavens and the Earth" (*Westminster Sermons*), 1866.

beggar died," we read, " and was carried by the angels into Abraham's bosom: the rich man also died, and in hell he lift up his eyes, being in torment."

If our Lord condescends for once to raise the veil from a part at least of the unseen world, how reverently should we look at what He deigns to show us. And we shall show our reverence best by taking our Lord's words exactly as they stand, and not turning them into any other words, however venerable such words may be from long custom or high authority. If the Son of God spake as never man spake, surely He knew best how to tell His own story, and convey His own lesson. His parable must be perfect in itself, and require no supplementing, much less explaining away by means of other texts. We should believe as much of the uninspired words of any great poet or philosopher. We should hold that as works of art they were complete in themselves, and must be studied as a whole, and allowed to tell their own tale. Let us, then, be at least as reverent to the words of the Incarnate God; and try to learn what we can from His parable as He Himself has spoken it. Let us indulge in no fancies of our own, but hear Scripture itself. In this case, as in all others, "to the law and to the testimony. If we speak not according to that Word there is no truth in us:" and if my interpretation differs from the usual one, it is because I try to follow our Lord's words exactly, and neither to alter them nor to add to them.

"There was a certain rich man," our Lord says, "who was clothed in purple and fine linen, and fared sumptuously every day," as he had from his wealth a right to do. We are not told that he was a gross sinner. If he neglected Lazarus, and gave him nothing, the parable does not make that a point of accusation against him. Nothing is said of his vices—nothing of his irreligion. He seems to have been simply an average selfish, luxurious man, such as we see every day.

"And there was a certain beggar named Lazarus, who was laid at his gate full of sores, and desiring to be fed with the crumbs which fell from the rich man's table : moreover the dogs came and licked his sores." Here, on the other hand, we are not told that Lazarus was a great saint. Nothing is said of his patience—nothing of his resignation. He is described simply as an object of pity. Remark, I beg, this fact. We have been told from childhood that Dives was a very bad man, and Lazarus a very good man, till we almost believe that our Lord says so. He says nothing of the kind.

"And it came to pass, that the beggar died, and was carried by the angels into Abraham's bosom."

We shall lose much of the deep pathos of those words if we overlook their exclusively Jewish character. The poor diseased outcast, the companion of the wild dogs in the street, who had often fancied that he was cut off from God, from his nation, finds in the next life that he was not cut off—that he was as much a child of Abraham as proud Pharisees and orthodox rabbis. In the bosom of the great Father of his nation he finds what he had so long needed—rest—rest as of a little child:—as many an outcast sleeping on our doorsteps, seemingly lost to God and society, may find likewise when his turn comes to die.

"And the rich man also died, and was buried; and in hell he lift up his eyes, being in torments." Certain divines, to carry out theories of their own, make a difference between Hades and Gehenna. Hades being merely the general place of departed spirits, Gehenna that of the endlessly lost. But that difference, very doubtful at best, will not hold good here: for the rich man is said not to be in Gehenna, but in Hades; the place whither David expected to *go*, but not to be *left;* the Hades whither Christ descended, and which He conquered and opened; the Hades which, according to St. John, He will destroy, and cast with Death into the lake of fire, to be burned up in the day when He shall destroy Death, and put all enemies under His feet. To this Hades, which simply means, like the Hebrew *Sheol* and the old Teutonic *Hela*, the hidden, covered, or unseen world, the rich man goes.

But he is in torment? Certainly. And what is the meaning of torment? Are we to take its meaning from its corruptions—from the cruel practice of the Roman law, which used torture to extract confession; or from the still more cruel practice of savages, who used torture as a mere means of giving pain—of indulging vindictive rage? Or are we to look at the original meaning of the word used in Scripture? That will be at once more reverent and more safe.

The rich man *basanizetai* (ὑπάρχων ἐν βασάνοις), says Scripture. That word is notoriously derived from *basanos*, a touchstone with which gold was tested. And therefore we must believe that Christ, the Lord of Words, used the word in its true sense, and that Dives was tormented to try if there was any gold in him which would abide the fire, and discover and bring out what good was left in him.

That this is the use of the fire of God is plain from St. Paul's words, for he tells us of a fire which shall try every man's work; and the worthless part, the wood, hay, and stubble, shall be burned up, while the valuable part, the gold and precious stones, shall endure; and the man himself be saved, yet so as by fire.[1] That this is God's method in this life we all know, or should know. We all know how affliction, sickness, even mere bodily pain, brings out the good in men. We talk of the purifying fire of affliction, and truly. Not that it has any power to atone for our sins—a mistake which lies at the root of the Romish doctrine of Purgatory—but that it does, as a fact, bring out whatever strength, whatever unselfishness there is left in us. We shall see whether it was so with the rich man. As was to be expected, it was not so with him at first. He sees Abraham afar off, and Lazarus in his bosom, and cries, "Father Abraham, have mercy on me, and send Lazarus, to dip the tip of his finger in water, and cool my tongue." His first cry is one of mere selfish desire for alleviation of unaccustomed bodily pain, mixed—and that is a hopeful sign—with the humiliating confession that Lazarus, the poor beggar, can and

[1] 1 Cor. iii. 11-15.

may be able to help him. Yet still he calls Abraham his "father." He appeals to Abraham's sympathy. He trusts that he is not cut off, even there, from the father of his nation. And he is not mistaken, though the tone of Abraham's answer is unexpected. It seems harsh and cruel, unless we take the parable in one way—and that is literally, as it stands.

"Son," says Abraham.—But, indeed, that first word is a mistranslation; it is not "Son," it is something far more tender which Abraham calls the rich man in his torment; even *tecknon*—my child. "My child, remember!"—He appeals to Dives's reason, to the sense of justice, as not dead in him even there. "Thou in thy lifetime receivedst thy good things, and likewise Lazarus evil things: but now he is comforted and thou art tormented." That is all the reason given. No word is said about his sins; no word about his neglect of Lazarus. Merely, the balance is to be made even between the two. Strange words! More terrible for the selfish and luxurious than any general doctrines about an endless punishment, to which no one believes that either he himself, or any one whom he ever met, is actually doomed. Strange words! which can only be reconciled with God's justice by the belief that punishment in the next life, as in this, is *a touchstone*, to try and to bring out the germ of good which is left in the man.

But besides all this, says Abraham, there is a great gulf fixed between them, which neither Dives nor Lazarus can cross.

From these words certain divines have argued that Dives is plainly doomed to stay for ever where he is. That notion is founded on another notion, which is nowhere to be found in Scripture, that there are only *two* states for men after death, and that if they are not where Lazarus was they must be where Dives was. Of that, I say, Scripture says not one word.

But let us take our Lord's words themselves, and consider; that these things must be interpreted spiritually, of spiritual and moral states. No one will say that Lazarus lay bodily in the bodily bosom of Abraham.

Then, by all rules of logic and reason, if we interpret one part of the parable spiritually we must interpret it all. And, then, not merely Abraham's bosom, but the fire and the gulf must indicate spiritual states and spiritual facts. Thus all becomes clear and reasonable, as well as just and hopeful.

Dives is, says Abraham, where he ought to be, in the state which his character had earned for him, and so is Lazarus; and they cannot cross to each other without changing their characters. Dives is in the state and place fit for selfish men. To come to him Lazarus must become selfish even as Dives is. And Dives, instead of giving himself up for lost, wailing and blaspheming as too many preachers would represent him as doing, takes Abraham's appeal to his reason patiently and reasonably, and begins thinking, not of himself, but of others. "I pray thee therefore, father Abraham, that thou wouldest send him to my father's house: for I have five brethren; that he may testify unto them, lest they come into this place of torment." Who shall deny that that is an improved state of mind?

Who shall deny that that is a gracious motion? Who shall deny that it is morally better for a man to think of saving his brothers from misery than merely to think of alleviating his own pain? But, then again, who shall deny that all moral improvement must proceed from God? Who shall deny, unless he wishes to incur a suspicion of the Pelagian heresy, that all gracious motions must proceed from the Spirit of God? Yet if the Spirit of God were working in Dives he was still under God's education — in God's schoolhouse, however severe. He cannot therefore be hopelessly and endlessly lost.

I say no more. That one fact surely settles the whole question, and we may have hope for Dives, and for many a poor soul besides.

But even that rational and humane request Abraham refuses to him whom he calls tenderly his "child"! "They have Moses and the prophets; let them hear them." *Them*—although, remember, the Old Testament says so little of the future state that it has been long an open question among divines whether its writers believed clearly in any future retribution at all. "Nay, father Abraham," replies the rich man, "but if one went unto them from the dead they will repent. And he said unto him, If they hear not Moses and the prophets, neither will they be persuaded though one rose from the dead."

Wonderful words! Words which only God Incarnate could have the wisdom or courage to have spoken; for what words have preachers in all ages been more slow to believe? How have they longed to call up one from the dead to frighten sinners by the horrors which he was enduring! How did they in the Middle Ages cover the walls of our churches with ghastly pictures of torment drawn from the Tartarus of Virgil and the Inferno of the Buddhists! How did they put heretics to dreadful deaths, confessedly to show their followers what they had to expect in the world to come! and how justifiable—how right was their method on their own ground! If the picture of Dives be that of one endlessly lost; and if that is to be the physical fate of the majority, or even of a few of the human race, what else ought a preacher to think of, speak of, preach of day and night, until he die, if by any means he may save one human being from that hideous doom? How strange, too, if this be the doom of the majority of the human race, is the silence of apostles and evangelists, except in the case of a few figurative and often disputed texts. How still more strange the utter silence of St. Paul, who never once throughout his Epistles alludes to the existence of such an Inferno as Dante has described in his too-immortal poem. But how most of all strange is our Lord's tone throughout the parable. Not a word of comment—a hint of pity—sympathy—horror. Did a merely human preacher describe to us the pains of the lost in such a tone, we should say that never had we heard a story told so coldly or so ill.

What then shall we say of it, when told by Him Who spake as never man spake, Who wept over Jerusalem, Who bore the infirmities and carried the sorrows of all mankind, Who stooped from the highest heaven to seek and to save that which was lost, Who was the Incarnate Charity, love, mercy, of God the Father of spirits? What shall we say but that, either as I hinted at first, the whole parable may apply simply to the fate of the Scribes and Pharisees, the generation of vipers; or that if it does not, there is even in this awful story, as in all Christ's words, a gospel, a good news of hope, a special revelation of the purposes of that God Who willeth that none should perish, but that all should be saved, and come like the rich man, if even through misery, to the knowledge of the truth?

A hope; but what hope? That their punishment will be at last remitted without repentance and amendment? Impossible. That would be to believe in the Romish purgatory. If the discipline is sent to amend them, disciplined they will be unless they amend. Their characters must change before they can change their state. Nay, if God's moral laws in the next life are at all like His moral laws in this life, they may, by refusing to amend, grow worse and worse, and therefore more and more miserable than ever. God grant that it will be so with no man; but that it *may* be so we cannot deny.

But for all who have departed in the faith and fear of Christ, for them we have no fear. They have chosen the good, and the good shall be its own ever-increasing reward. They have chosen the light, and in God's light they shall ever see clearer and clearer light. Their souls have tended upward, while on earth, to God who is their source; and of them it is written, "They shall mount up with wings as eagles; they shall run, and not be weary; they shall walk, and not faint," till they return to that God from whom they came. Of them it is written that they shall go from strength to strength until before the God of gods appeareth every one of them in Zion. Of them it is written, that beholding as in a glass the glory of the Lord they shall be changed into His likeness from glory to glory. They have chosen the upward path, and God will lead them on it. They have fought on earth in Christ's warfare against evil, and their reward shall be to enter more and more fully, as the ages roll on, into the joy of perfect duty, perfect beneficence, perfect unselfishness, perfect usefulness, which is the joy of their Lord.

Commemoration of the Blessed Dead

"'Ye are come,' said St. Paul to the Hebrews, 'to the spirits of just men made perfect.'

"Into the presence of this noble company we too have come: even nobler company. . . . For more than 1800 years have passed since those words were written: and how many thousands of just men and women, pure, noble, tender, wise, beneficent, have graced the earth since then, and left their mark upon mankind, and helped forward the coming of the Father's Kingdom. Let us rejoice in the thought . . . and give God thanks for all His servants departed in His faith and fear. Let us rejoice in the thought that we know not how many they are; only that they are an innumerable company, out of all tongues and nations, whom no man can number. Let us rejoice that the goodly company in whose presence we stand can be limited and defined by no mortal man, or school of men: but only by Him from whom, with the Father, proceeds for ever the Holy Spirit, the inspirer of all Good."

C. K., *Westminster Sermons.*

". . . And he—where is he now? If it were altogether wise and safe to indulge our fancy about the state of souls in bliss, might we not ask, To what unknown heights has he not risen? He whose life was one of spotless purity, of sacred horror and pity for all things mean, and false, and foul—to what realms of perfect purity is he risen, washed from all earthly stains in the mystic blood of Christ? He whose whole life was a search after truth, wisdom, beauty, law—what may he not be seeing now, not as on earth, through a glass darkly, but in the full inspiration of the Spirit of God? What divine truths, divine wisdom, divine beauty, divine laws, may he not be beholding now, in that intellectual world, which is the perfect and eternal pattern of the mind of God? He whose whole life was sacrificed to duty—what duties may be allotted to him now, nobler far than even those which he performed on earth? He who lived to do good, in his own family and in every good work—what good may he not be doing now—what royal labour may not be intrusted to him in that world in which all live to God, and in God, and for God? We know not and we need not know. But Scripture and reason both make it likely that the spirits of the blest at least know, and it may be help those whom they have left behind on earth. Our hearts tell us so, and all the arguments in the world will not drive from us the devout imagination, even if it be nothing more—which God forbid. . . ."

C. K., *MS. Sermon on the Death of the Prince Consort.*

SERMON IV

Commemoration of the Blessed Dead[1]

"If any man serve me, let him follow me; and where I am, there shall also my servant be: if any man serve me, him will my Father honour."—JOHN xii. 26.

E do not in the Church of England now pray for the dead. We are not absolutely, if at all, forbidden by Scripture to do so. But we believe that they are where they ought to be. That they are gone to a perfectly just world, in which there are none of the mistakes, confusion, wrong and oppression of this world; in which they will therefore receive the due reward of their deeds done in the body, whether they

---

[1] This is the latter part of a funeral sermon on the death of the Right Hon. Thomas Erskine, 1865.

be good or evil ; that they are in the hands of a perfectly just God, who rewardeth every man according to his work. It seems to us therefore unnecessary, and, so to speak, an impertinence towards God, to pray for those who are in the unseen world of spirits, exactly in that state which they have deserved.

But if we may not pray for the dead, there is no reason why we may not give thanks for them, if we knew them in this life to have been such that we may have a reasonable hope that, now they have departed hence, they rest in God. We have a right to say, in the Burial Service, that God has of His great mercy taken to Himself their souls. We have a right to give God hearty thanks, that He has delivered them out of the miseries of this sinful world. We have a right to hear, with the ears of faith, a voice from heaven saying to us—" Blessed are the dead which die in the Lord : even so, saith the Spirit ; for they rest from their labours." This we have a right to say when we commit their bodies to the grave, in the belief that their souls, now that they are delivered from the burden of the flesh, are in joy and felicity, living with God for ever.

But more. We need not say this once and for all, blessed as is that privilege. We may say it again and again; and again and again give God thanks for them. We may say it whenever we think of them. We may say it whenever we look at the good deeds which they have left behind them. We may say it—and more, we are bound to say it—whenever we come to Holy Communion. Then, in that great prayer for the Church Militant—for all Christ's servants who are still fighting here on earth, in God's war against evil—after praying for kings and rulers, for bishops and clergy, for all Christian people, that they each and all may do their duty where God has put them, in the name and for the sake of God; after praying God to comfort and succour those on whom misery and want and wrong, and any other of the bitter fruits of sin lie heavily;—after all this, it is our duty and our right to look up from earth to heaven—from those who are still struggling to those whose warfare is accomplished; from those who are still suffering, to those who have suffered enough—and to commemorate the righteous dead, and bless God's Holy Name for all His servants departed this life in His faith and fear, beseeching Him to give us grace so to follow their good examples, that with them we may be partakers of His heavenly kingdom.

We may do this, for two reasons, which our Lord Himself gives us. "If any man serve me, let him follow me; and where I am, there shall also my servant be." If any man serve Me: not merely with service of the lips, or with outward observances—these are well. But a man may do this, and yet not be Christ's true servant. To be Christ's true servant, he must follow Christ. And in what? "Let him take up his cross," says our Lord, "and follow me." To take up the cross means, in the minds of most persons, to suffer patiently under affliction. And it is a true and sound meaning. But it means more. Why did Christ take up His cross? Why did He suffer affliction? Not for affliction's sake, or the cross's sake, as if suffering were a good thing in itself. No. But that He might thereby *do good;* that the world through Him might be saved; that He might do good, at whatever cost and pain to Himself. And so do Christ's true servants who take up their cross and follow Him in the work of self-sacrifice and benevolence. Of them Christ says, "Where I am, there shall my servant be also."

But more. He says of such—"If any man serve me, him will my Father honour." What words are these! Shall the Creator honour the creature? The sinless God honour sinful man? Shall He who charges His angels with folly, and in whose sight the very heavens are not clean, He who can be satisfied with no perfection short of His own perfect perfectness—shall He stoop to honour, to look with anything like esteem on the paltry goodness of even the best of men, the poor holiness of the holiest saint?

It is difficult to understand, and difficult to believe, unless perhaps we look on the matter in this light—that it is the pleasure which a father takes in his children. He brought them into being, that they might be like Himself. For that purpose He made them His children, that they might copy His character and be, however dimly and imperfectly, what Christ the only-begotten Son of God was clearly and perfectly, the likeness of His glory and image of His person. And therefore He honours, looks with esteem and pleasure, on even the smallest effort of theirs to be like Him, their Heavenly Father. So it is not they themselves that He honours, but Christ in them; not their righteousness which He esteems, but His own righteousness in them—the fruits of His Spirit.

And if He honours them, my friends, shall not we honour them likewise? We may not, as our forefathers did, blindly though lovingly, worship them as mediators and lesser gods—pray to them, instead of to that Father in heaven to whose throne of grace we may all come boldly through Jesus Christ—or believe that their relics will work miracles in our behalf. This we may not do. The times of that ignorance in our forefathers God winked at instead of punishing, because their mistake was one of reverence and love, and honest admiration of goodness and holiness—a good feeling overstrained. He has long since commanded men to repent of that, and to worship Him alone, and no more to honour the creature instead of the Creator. But though we may not honour the creature instead of the Creator, we may honour the Creator in His creature, honour God in those who have lived godly and godlike lives. And when they have passed away from among us—souls endued by God with manifold virtues and precious gifts of grace—we may give God thanks and say:—"These, O God, are the fruits of Thy Spirit. Thou honourest them in heaven with Thy approving smile; we will honour them on earth, not merely with our lips, but in our lives. What these persons were, we too might be if we were as true as they to the inspirations of Thy Holy Spirit. Help us to honour their memories, as Thou and as they would have us do, by following their example; by setting them before us,—and not them only, but every holy and noble personage of whom we have ever heard, as dim likenesses of Christ—even as Christ is the likeness of Thee."

And above all, in Holy Communion.—[1] Shall we not recollect them there? And give thanks for them there, at that Holy Table at which the Church Triumphant and the Church Militant meet in the Communion of Saints? Where Christ is they are, and therefore if Christ be there may not they be there likewise? May not they be near us, though unseen, like us claiming their share in the eternal sacrifice—like us partaking of that spiritual Body and Blood, which is as much the life of saints in heaven as it is of penitent sinners upon earth? May it not be so? It is a mystery into which we will not look too far. But this at least is certain, that they are with Him where He is.

[1] *Vide* Sermon on "All Saints' Day" and "Presence in Absence" Volume *All Saints' Day and other Sermons*).

The Resurrection of the Body

"The Creed says, 'I believe in the Resurrection of the flesh.' I believe that we, each of us, as human beings, men and women, shall have a share in that glorious day; not merely as ghosts and disembodied spirits, but as real live human beings, with new bodies of our own, on a new earth, under a new heaven. 'Therefore,' David says, 'my flesh shall rest in hope;' not merely my soul, my ghost, but my flesh. For the Lord, who not only died but rose again with His body, shall raise our bodies according to His mighty working, and then the whole manhood of us—body, soul, and spirit—shall have our perfect consummation and bliss in His eternal and everlasting glory." C. K., *National Sermons.*

"Christianity alone deprives old age of its bitterness, making it the gate of heaven. Our bodies will fade and grow weak . . . in close expectation of that Resurrection of the flesh which is the great promise of Christianity—no miserable fancies about 'pure souls escaped from matter'—but bodies, *our* bodies, beloved, beautiful, ministers to us in all our joys, sufferers with us in all our sorrows—yea, our very own selves raised up again to live and love in a manner inconceivable from its perfection." C. K., *MSS. Letters.*

"Day and night I look forward with quiet certainty of hope, believing, though I can see but little daylight, that all this tangled web will resolve itself into golden threads of twined, harmonious life, guiding both us, and those we love, together, through this life to that Resurrection of the flesh, when we shall at last know the reality and the fulness of life and love. Even so come, Lord Jesus!" C. K., *MSS. Letters.*

"No! I can wait:
Another body!—Ah, new limbs are ready,
Free, pure, instinct with soul through every nerve,
Kept for us in the treasuries of God!"
C. K., *Santa Maura.*

SERMON V

The Resurrection of the Body

"How are the dead raised up? and with what body do they come?"—1 COR. xv. 35.

EN, even godly men, are often puzzled and perplexed with doubts about the resurrection of the dead. Men ask now, as the Corinthians did in St. Paul's time :—" How are the dead raised up, and with what body do they come?" How, they asked, will each man at the day of judgment find his own body, and enter into it again? His bones may be scattered over the face of the earth. His body may have ceased to be a body at all; it may have turned again to its dust—have become part of a plant or a tree root in a different country

hundreds of years after his death, and so on for ages, change after change, till it will be impossible for each man to have back his own body again. How, then, they say, can we believe in the resurrection of the dead?

I do not speak here of scoffers and scorners, who turn the doctrine of the resurrection of the dead into ridicule, and make a mock of things which, even if they were not true, occupy so deeply important a place in human history that they should be only thought of carefully, and patiently, and reverently. I speak of well-meaning persons, godly persons who are puzzled and troubled in mind when they think about the resurrection of the dead, and how it can possibly happen. Now, to them, as well as to the insolent scoffers, St. Paul says, in his great chapter on this subject, the fifteenth of his First Epistle to the Corinthians, "Thou fool!"—not bitterly or angrily, but, as it were, with a kindly smile; rebuking them lovingly for being so stupid as not to open their eyes to all that is going on round them day and night, and see that in every field and garden

THE RESURRECTION OF THE BODY

there are sights enough—not to *explain* the resurrection of the dead, but to show that it is reasonable and possible, and like to, although greater than, what we see going on in Nature every day.

Why torment your minds, he asks, with the thought :—" Shall I when I rise again be able to get back the very same particles which now make up my body, though they have turned to dust and been scattered to the winds?" If you have your own body, says St. Paul, it matters not what particles the body may be made up of. It may be made of quite different materials from what it is now, and yet be your body. You see for yourselves that all flesh is not the same flesh—that the bodies of men and of beasts are not made in the same form as those of birds; or those of birds in the same as those of fish; or those of fish as those of worms and insects; and yet they are all bodies. Why should not your body, when you rise, be as different from what it is now, as the body of a man is from the body of a worm? Your flesh, says St. Paul, is not really your body; it is only the stuff of which your body happens now to be put together. It is no more your body than the bricks are the house. Heaping all the bricks in the world together would not make a house. What makes a building into a house, is its being put together by certain rules, in a certain shape, for a certain purpose, namely, for men to live in; and whether it be built of brick, or wood, or iron, or any other material, it is a house still, provided it be of such a shape and so made that men can live in it.

So with your bodies, says St. Paul. Your body is that thing through which you speak and think, and enjoy, and work. And if you can do that with your body it will be a good body, however it may be made; whether as it is made now, or made still better—stronger, swifter, less liable to confuse you, and tire you, and make you stupid and out of temper; less liable to decay and die, more able to enjoy what is pleasant, more able to work and do the business to which your Heavenly Father will set you in the next life. Never mind what your new body will be made of;

but be sure that it will be a right good and serviceable body. Lift up your eyes, says St. Paul, and look at the wonderful boundless variety of things in the world round you—plants and leaves, beasts and birds, sun, moon and stars; each star, as learned men tell us, thousands and tens of thousands though there are of them, different from each other. Each of these has a body, a shape, a rule, a law given it by God; and each is fitted by God's wisdom for the work which He has given it to do. Why do you doubt, then, His power and His wisdom? He gives bodies to each thing which you see around you, from the sun which shines and will shine for ages and ages in heaven, to the butterfly which comes out in the sunshine with a new body, formed just as beautifully and delicately as your own body; and which yet is not intended to live a month, but may perhaps die before sunset, leaving behind it, not butterflies like itself, but eggs, which are quite unlike it in shape, and which will lie dead all the winter on some leaf or branch till spring brings them to life in a new shape—not as butterflies, but as caterpillars—ugly creeping things, feeding on the leaves of trees. You would not fancy that these creatures could ever become butterflies; and yet what happens to them? In autumn they completely change their shape again into grubs, something still uglier. They bury themselves in the ground at the tree root, or hang themselves up in cracks and corners. They seem to die—they do really die in one sense. And all the winter through there is no motion in them; they can neither see nor feed. Only little by little they get a slight power of moving, though they cannot stir from their place. Are they like butterflies? And yet whence come every summer all those troops of beautiful creatures which we admire, flitting about from flower to flower, sucking the sweet honey, sporting in the sunshine, with wings so wonderfully painted that even Solomon in all his glory was not arrayed like one of them?

Where has it come from, that beautiful butterfly? Yesterday it was the ugly, hard, motionless grub, which lay in the earth all the winter through. Last summer it was the crawling, greedy caterpillar, devouring the tree leaves. Last spring it was the little dead egg, glued tight to the branch of a tree. Three times it has changed; three times it has seemed to die; three times it seemed to become more and more ugly as it changed: and yet that very same one individual living creature, which was in turn egg, caterpillar, and grub, is now the glorious butterfly spreading its beauty to the sun.

Even so is the resurrection of the dead. Like the caterpillar, we are buried in the earth—sown in corruption, in dishonour, in weakness. Like the butterfly, which is raised to a new life of joy, and beauty, and swiftness, we shall be raised in incorruption, in glory, in power. Seems it to us a thing impossible that God should raise the dead? Does not every poor insect which flies past us, beautiful at last after all its ugly changes, rather preach to us, saying, "Is anything too hard for God's power? and is anything too hard for God's love?" Let us rather ask, "Is it not impossible that God should *not* raise the dead?" If He so clothes the poor crawling worm—if He cares for the insect which must die to-morrow—if He condescends to spend all that wisdom, all that love, upon a fly—how much more will He clothe you, care for you, spend His wisdom and His love on you, O ye of little faith!

But St. Paul speaks of another change in connection with the resurrection of the dead, in which the insects cannot, as far as we see, partake at all—though, after all, we know nothing of what God in the depths of His love may have in store even for the beasts that perish.

Man's body, St. Paul says, is sown a natural body; it is raised a spiritual body. Now what the difference between a natural body and a spiritual body is, we are not yet wise enough to know. Only this we know. In nature — that is, in the world around us—all things decay and die at last, as these natural bodies of ours which we have now must one day die. But spirit cannot die. Therefore those new spiritual bodies of ours will never die.

And another thing we may be sure of regarding the spiritual bodies with which we shall rise again; and that is, in Whose right, and by Whose power, and for Whose sake, these spiritual bodies will be given us—by the power and for the sake of our Lord Jesus Christ.

"There is a natural body, and there is a spiritual body. And so it is written—The first man Adam was made a living soul, the last Adam"—that is, the Lord Jesus—"a quickening Spirit. The first man is of the earth, earthy; the second man is the Lord from heaven." There is the warrant of our birthright. There is the ground of our full assurance of hope. Adam, our natural forefather, was of the earth, earthy; subject to death like the animals. But he was not the real head and lord of us. No;—Man was created in the likeness of the Lord Jesus Christ. From that likeness he fell by sin, and became subject to death, like the animals; and as the world went on, all mankind became more and more like the beasts that perish, and spiritually dead in trespasses and sins.

Then came the true Head of Man—the

Lord in whose likeness man was made at first. And He redeemed us again. He lived as a man; He died as a man. But then He showed that men were meant to do more than merely live and die—for He rose again from the dead. The bands of death had no power over Him. It was not possible that He should be held down by them; for He was very God of very God, eternal, immortal. Yet as He proved that God could take man's nature on Him, so He proved that man was not made in the likeness of the beasts that perish, nor even in the likeness of Adam who died :—that death was only the consequence of sin; that man was really made in the likeness of God; that by faith in the Lord his God he could rise out of his sins, rise to the glory and honour which God had intended for him; rise from death itself, rise, with a new and glorious and spiritual body, as his Lord Jesus Christ, the new Adam, had risen before him.

This, then, is the ground of our hope. Hope for ourselves, hope too for every one who has departed in faith and trust in the Lord, the new Adam—however dim and weak that faith may have been. The Lord Jesus Christ rose. The Lord Jesus Christ put on, when He rose, a new and glorious body, which was yet the very same body which He had had all along, with the print of the nails in His most blessed hands and feet, the print of the spear in His most holy side. And therefore what He did for Himself He can do for us who are made in His likeness at our birth, and renewed day by day into His likeness by faith and repentance and the grace of His Spirit. He can do it, for He is almighty in power. He will do it, for He is boundless in love. He must do it, for He has given us in His sacraments everlasting warrants of His promises. He will change these bodies of our humiliation, that they may be like unto His glorious body, according to the mighty working by which He can subdue all things unto Himself. Death,[1] the stubbornest and the strongest enemy which He has to fight against, He

---

[1] *Vide* "The Victory of Life" (*Water of Life Sermons*), and "Consider the Lilies" (*Discipline and other Sermons*).

will conquer last. And He will conquer it. He has conquered it already for Himself, and therefore He can conquer it for us also. And then, in the new heavens and the new earth—in which righteousness shall dwell, and only the saints shall rule—where there shall be no more curse, nor sorrow, but God shall wipe away tears from all eyes—shall be brought to pass the saying that is written—" Death shall be swallowed up of victory. O death, where is thy sting? O grave, where is thy victory? The sting of death is sin ; and the strength of sin is the law. But thanks be to God, which giveth us the victory, through our Lord Jesus Christ. Therefore, my beloved brethren, be ye steadfast, unmovable, always abounding in the work of the Lord, forasmuch as ye know that your labour is not in vain in the Lord." Amen.

The Hope of Life

"'Brother,' said the abbot, 'make ready for me the divine elements, that I may consecrate them.' And he asking the reason therefore, the saint replied, 'That I may partake thereof with all my brethren before I depart hence. For know assuredly that within the seventh day I shall migrate to the celestial mansions. For this night stood by me in a dream those two women whom I love, and for whom I pray, the one clothed in a white, the other in a ruby-coloured garment, and holding each other by the hand, who said to me, "*That life after death is not such a one as you fancy:* come, therefore, and behold what it is like."'"

C. K., *Hypatia*, last chapter.

"The world which shall be hereafter—ay, which shall be! Believe it, toil-worn worker—God made you love beautiful things only because He intends to give you your fill of them. That pictured face . . . is lovely, but lovelier still shall the wife of thy bosom be when she meets thee on the Resurrection Morn! Those baby-cherubs in the old Italian painting—how gracefully they flutter and sport among the soft clouds, full of rich young life and baby joy! Yes, beautiful indeed, but just such a one at this very moment is that once pining, deformed child of thine, over whose death-cradle thou wast weeping a month ago; now a child-angel, whom thou shalt meet again never to part! Those landscapes too—painted by loving, wise old Claude 200 years ago, are still as fresh as ever. How still the meadows are! how pure and free that vault of deep blue sky! no wonder that thy worn heart as thou lookest cries out, 'O for the wings of a dove!' Ah! but gayer meadows and bluer skies await thee *in the world to come,* that fairyland made real, 'the new heavens and the new earth,' which God has prepared for the pure and the loving, the just and the brave, who have conquered in the sore fight of life."

C. K., "Thoughts in the National Gallery"—
True Words for Brave Men, 1848.

SERMON VI

The Hope of Life

"Now the God of hope fill you with all joy and peace in believing, that ye may abound in hope, through the power of the Holy Ghost."—ROM. xv. 13.

HAT was the Hope that St. Paul spoke of to the Romans when he said these words to them, "Whatsoever things were written aforetime were written for our learning, that we through patience and comfort of the Scriptures might have hope"? Hope? What hope? Hope about what? Hope of what?

Now the answer to this question we must find in the Old Testament rather than in the New. I do not mean to say that the New Testament is not full of hope. God forbid!

You cannot read a chapter of it fairly without seeing that it is the most hopeful book in the world—a gospel of good news for sinful men. All I mean is, that St. Paul was not speaking of the New Testament, when he spoke of the Scriptures through which we might have hope, because at that time the New Testament was not written. Probably neither of the four Gospels, nor the Acts of the Apostles, nor most of the Epistles were written till some years after this Epistle to the Romans. When St. Paul speaks of the Scriptures, therefore, he seems always to mean the Jewish Scriptures, which we call the Old Testament.

Thus we see in this very chapter he goes on to say that Christ confirmed the promises made to the Fathers, *i.e.* to the old Jews, and especially to Abraham; and then he quotes texts from the Old Testament, and especially from the glorious prophecies of the great evangelical prophet, Isaiah. Therefore it is to the Old Testament we must look first to see what "hope" St. Paul spoke of, and surely to the very prophecy he quotes from Isaiah, " There shall be a root of Jesse, and he that shall rise to reign over the Gentiles; in him shall the Gentiles trust." After which he adds, "Now the God of hope fill you with all joy and peace in believing, that ye may abound in hope, through the power of the Holy Ghost."

What does this prophecy promise to us? Let us read Isaiah's own words.[1] "And there shall come forth a rod out of the stem of Jesse, and a Branch shall grow out of his roots: and the spirit of the Lord shall rest upon him, the spirit of wisdom and understanding, the spirit of counsel and might, the spirit of knowledge and of the fear of the Lord; and shall make him of quick understanding in the fear of the Lord: and he shall not judge after the sight of his eyes, neither reprove after the hearing of his ears: but with righteousness shall he judge the poor, and reprove with equity for the meek of the earth. . . . And righteousness shall be the girdle of his loins, and faithfulness the girdle of his reins."

What, I say, does this prophecy promise

[1] Isa. xi. 1-5.

to us? A king—a king of the stem of Jesse, that is, of the House of David. It was a great thing for the Jews that Christ should be one of their nation, and of their royal family likewise: but that is not so great a matter to us. What is a great matter to us, a matter of infinite hope and joy, is the character of the Kingship—that Christ is a good and perfect King who shall set the world right, a King who shall reign in righteousness. Yes, this prophecy we feel is true. It *must* be true. It answers to something in the heart of every humane and thoughtful man—of every one who has ever looked sadly at the sin and misery of the world, and said:—"All this ought not to be, and therefore it will not be. It will surely end some day, and the world will be set right." Deep in the heart of man is planted the hope that the world will not be always wicked, always confused, always subject to war, and plague, and famine, and misery; that better times will come, that a heavenly King shall rule in righteousness over a new heaven and a new earth. Philosophy did not put that belief into men's hearts, and philosophy cannot take it away: but as, I believe, the Spirit of God put it into men's hearts, so the Spirit of God will not let men lose that precious hope as long as there is a crime or a sorrow upon earth.

The old pagans had this hope, for God had put it into their hearts—dimly indeed, and mixed with fables—but there it was; ready for the apostles and missionaries of the Church to work on when they came to preach the Gospel to them. The Romans, for instance, while they were yet heathens, had, many of them, no doubt, heard the old fable of Astrea, the goddess of heavenly justice, the daughter of Zeus and Themis —that is, of Religion and Law—how once she dwelt among men, and taught them in the Golden Age, while all were good. And how at last Astrea was wearied with their sins, and fled away to heaven: but how again she would return from heaven at last, to fill the world with righteousness once more. And surely, when St. Paul preached to these same Romans of Christ coming in glory to abolish sin and death and to reign in righteousness, they would say:—"This is the truth, after which we had been feeling in the dark. All that we had fancied from the old fable is true, and more, far more. And therefore we will have hope."

Our own heathen forefathers, too, had their dream about it—half true, half false. They believed, the wisest of them, that a time would come of exceeding wickedness—an Iron Age they called it, an Axe Age, a Sword Age, when every man should hate and slay his brother; for Baldur, the God of Light, was dead, and had descended into hell, and therefore men would grow worse and worse till the end—till Ragnarok, the twilight of the gods,—when earth and heaven, sun and stars, should be burned up, and the gods themselves should perish with the heavens. And afterwards? Afterwards would arise out of the sea another earth, lovely and green, with pleasant fields where grain should spring unsown; and a new sun should rise in heaven, fairer than the old; and Baldur, the God of

Light, should rise again out of hell, and rule over that new earth, and it should be peopled with new human beings, and there should be no more war, nor sin, nor woe.

One must see at once how such dreams as these, dim and confused though they were, would make the people ready to receive the truth when it was preached to them; and how they would rejoice in this prophecy of Isaiah, and "through patience and comfort of the Scriptures have hope."

There are other old stories, too, which show how apt men are to cling to the hope, that somehow, somewhen, somewhere, God will set all things right once more. The old Britons, whom we English conquered and drove out of the land fifteen hundred years ago, had their fable too which gave them hope—how that their great King Arthur was not really dead, but slept a charmed sleep in the Isle of Avalon; and how he should awake at last to set them free, and rule righteously over the land. That was but a fable, and has come to nought: but still it was true to the best instincts of human nature, true to the promise of God, whose kingdom, verily, shall one day come, and His will be done on earth as it is in heaven.

The old Germans likewise had their dream of hope—and, indeed, many of the countryfolk among them have it still. They tell of their great and good Emperor, Frederick Barbarossa, who died fighting against the Saracens in the East, that he might win back from them the Holy Sepulchre at Jerusalem, in which our Lord was laid. They say that he is not really dead; but that he sits asleep in a cave in the mountains, waiting for the last day, with a table of stone before him—and how, before the last day, he will awake and come forth, and punish all cruel tyrants, and rid poor people of their oppressors, and do justice and judgment throughout the empire, in the name of Christ and of God. That, too, is a dream and a fable: but God forbid that we should laugh at such. They are all, as it were, parables—not true themselves, but teaching the truth—keeping alive in men's hearts the belief that Christ will set the world right one day; and leading them to the true light of the Bible, so that in spite of all the misrule, and sin, and misery of the world, by patience and comfort of the Scriptures they may have hope.

Now one point in these stories which helped men to believe the prophecies of Scripture is that they, like the prophecies of Scripture, are not *selfish*. What do I mean? I mean this. The men who repeated those stories did not value them merely for their own sake, but for the sake of those who would come after them, of their children's children and of mankind. Long before the evil times in which they lived were over, and the good time come, they would be dead, and their souls would have gone they knew not whither. But they would have died in faith, not having received the promises. And because they died in faith, they would have died in hope. They could delight in the thought that the world would be good one day, even if it was bad then—that their children's children would be happy, even if they themselves were miserable. And so it is with the prophecies of the Old Testament. The fathers, says St. Paul, died in faith, *not* having received the promises. They believed that their children's children would receive them some day, and that was enough for them. And more, because they were inspired by the Holy Spirit of God, they looked for a time when the Gentiles should receive them too—the Gentile heathen, men not of their own blood, their enemies, who were unclean, and with whom they would not even eat. Yet those Gentiles, too, in spite of the wall of separation which parted them from the Jews as sharply as if they were not men at all, but some other kind of creatures—those Gentiles they believed would be blessed some day by God, through Christ. The heathen would glorify God for His mercy; the heathen would rejoice with His people; a King would arise to reign in righteousness over Gentiles as well as Jews, and in Him should the Gentiles trust.

Then would be fulfilled to the heathen all, and more than all, those dreams and fancies about a good King from heaven, and a new earth in which dwelleth righteousness, which had been stirring in their minds—perhaps God put them into their minds, at least God left them there. He did not despise those fancies, silly and ignorant as they often were; they were all hints, and signs, and witnesses for Christ, the true King and Saviour. As St. Paul says,[1] "God hath made of one blood all nations of men to dwell on the face of the earth, and hath determined the times before appointed, and the bounds of their habitation; that they should seek the Lord, if haply they might feel after him, and find him, though he be not far from any one of us: for in him we live, and move, and have our being; as certain also of your own poets have said, For we also are his offspring."

Be sure that all those hopes will come true in God's good time, at the second coming of our Lord Jesus Christ, and sin and sorrow shall come to an end under the rule of Him, our righteous King.

Of the times and the seasons of that great day knoweth no man; none save God the

[1] Acts xvii. 26-28.

Father. Of the manner and the way of that great and blessed change knoweth no man—as it is written, "Eye hath not seen, nor ear heard, nor hath it entered into the heart of man to conceive, what God hath prepared for those who love him." But it will come when God shall will, and as God shall will. The tabernacle of God shall be with men, and He will dwell with them, and they shall be His people, and He their God. And God shall wipe away all tears from their eyes, and there shall be no more death, neither sorrow, nor crying, neither shall there be any more pain, for the former things are passed away. And He that sitteth on the throne hath said, "Behold, I make all things new."

Then shall be fulfilled all the hopes of those who have longed to see justice and peace upon the earth. Then shall be answered the prayers of all who have cried to Christ, "Lord, how long ere Thou come, and arise upon the dark earth, a Sun of Righteousness with healing in Thy wings?" Then all those shall be comforted whose hearts have ached over the misery and

pain and sin which they see around them in this sinful world. Then all those shall have their reward who have done their part towards lessening that sin and misery ; who have fed the hungry, clothed the naked, comforted the mourners, taught the ignorant, righted the opprest. To them shall be said in that day:—
" Come, ye blessed children of God, who have tried to copy Christ on earth. Come and see Christ Himself do for this sinful world what you tried, each in your place and state, to do. Come and see Him make all things new. Come and enter into the joy of your Lord—the unspeakable joy of seeing sin and misery banished for ever out of God's universe, and the whole creation filled with righteousness, and peace, and joy in the Holy Ghost."

Even so, come quickly, Lord Jesus. Amen.

"I am startled by hearing a man talk of the eternity of hell-fire, who believes the Athanasian Creed, that there is but one Eternal. If so, then this fire is the fire of God—yea, is God Himself, whom the Scriptures formally identify with that fire. And if so it must be a fire of purification, not of mere useless torment; it must be a spiritual and not a physical fire, and its eternity must be a good, a blessed, an ever useful one; and amenable to the laws which God has revealed concerning the rest of His attributes, and especially to the great law 'when the wicked man turneth he shall save his soul alive.' This eternal law no metaphors of fire and brimstone can abrogate. . . ."

C. K., *Letters and Memories.*

". . . As for the question of 'evil,' on which I know as little as all the rest of mankind, I agree with you on the whole . . . but men can and do resist God's will, and break the law, which is appointed for them, and so punish themselves by getting into disharmony with their own constitution and that of the universe; just as a wheel in a piece of machinery punishes itself when it gets out of gear. I may be wrong, but so it seems to me. My conception of God's Providence meanwhile is, that He is, by a divine irony, lovingly baffling all the lawlessness and self-will of the spirits whom He has made, and turning it into means for their education, as a father does with his children. Whether they take the lesson which He offers, depends on them; but the chances would seem, I should have said, to be in favour of God's proving too good an instructor to lose finally any of His pupils. The world thinks differently, you know: but I am content to be in the minority, for the few years of life which remain to me, to find myself, I trust, in the majority, when I come into the other world. . . ."

C. K., *Letters and Memories*, Vol. I., 1852.

Appendix

"As to the mediæval conception of Heaven and Hell, educated men are asking more and more. Heaven and Hell—the Spiritual World—are they merely invisible places in space, which may become visible hereafter? or are they not rather the moral world—the world of right and wrong? Love and righteousness—is not that the Heaven itself wherein God dwells? Hatred and sin—is not that Hell itself, wherein dwells all that is opposed to God? . . . We do not deny—they say—that the wages of sin is death. We do not deny the necessity of punishment—the certainty of punishment. We see it working awfully enough around us in this life; we believe that it may work in still more awful forms in the life to come. Only tell us not that it must be endless, and thereby destroy its whole purpose and (as we think) its whole morality. We too believe in an eternal fire; but we believe its existence to be—not a curse, but a Gospel and a blessing, seeing that that fire is God Himself, who taketh away the sins of the world, and of whom it is therefore written, 'Our God is a consuming fire.'"

C. K., *The Shaking of Heaven and Earth*, preached at Whitehall, 1866.

"As soon as you introduce priority and posteriority of Time, and not merely of moral relation, you get involved in contradiction. It is that Lockite superstition of cognising everything, even God Himself, as under the conditions of Time, which makes all the difficulty nowadays. Though one must not lay the blame on Locke, Calvin is, perhaps, the offender. The whole Calvinistic theology—demonology call it—is based on the fallacy that God is comprehended by Time, and that He has not made Time (in making the universe), but is made, they can't say how—by Time."

C. K., *Letters and Memories*, 1852.

"Eternity does not mean merely some future endless duration, but that ever-present *moral* world, governed by ever-living and absolutely necessary laws, in which we and all spirits are now; and in which we should be equally, whether Time and Space, extension and duration, and the whole material universe to which they belong became nothing this moment, or lasted endlessly."

C. K., 1854.

APPENDIX

LETTER to T. COOPER.[1]

May 9, 1857.

"ABOUT *endless torment*. (Keep that expression distinct from *eternal*, which has been mixed up with it, the former being what the popular creed really holds.) You may say,

"1. Historically, that

"*a.* The doctrine occurs nowhere in the Old Testament, nor any hint of it. The expression, in the end of Isaiah, about the fire unquenched, and the worm not dying, is plainly of the dead corpses of men upon the physical earth, in the valley of Hinnom, or Gehenna, where the offal of Jerusalem was burned perpetually. Enlarge on this, as it is the passage which our Lord quotes, and by it the meaning of His words must be primarily determined.

"*b.* The doctrine of endless torment was, as a historical fact, brought back from Babylon by the Rabbis. It was a very ancient primary doctrine of

---

[1] Thomas Cooper was at that time lecturing to working men in London.—*Vide* whole letter in *Letters and Memories*, Early Edition, Vol. I., 1877.

the Magi, an appendage of their fire-kingdom of Ahriman, and may be found in the old Zends, long prior to Christianity.

"*c.* St. Paul accepts nothing of it as far as we can tell, never making the least allusion to the doctrine.

"*d.* The Apocalypse simply repeats the imagery of Isaiah and of our Lord; but asserts, distinctly, the non-endlessness of torture, declaring that in the consummation not only death, but hell, shall be cast into the lake of fire.

"*e.* The Christian Church has never really held it exclusively till now. It remained quite an open question till the age of Justinian, 530, and significantly enough, as soon as, 200 years before that, endless torment for the heathen became a popular theory, Purgatory sprang up synchronously by the side of it, as a relief for the conscience and reason of the Church.

"*f.* Since the Reformation it has been an open question in the English Church, and the philosophical Platonists, of the sixteenth and seventeenth centuries, always considered it as such.

"*g.* The Church of England, by the deliberate expunging of the 42d Article, which affirmed endless punishment, has declared it authoritatively to be open.

"*h.* It is so, in fact. Neither Mr. Maurice, I, nor any others who have denied it, can be dispossessed or proceeded against legally in any way whatsoever.

"Exegetically, you may say, I think, *a*, That the meanings of the word αἰών and αἰώνιος have little or nothing to do with it, even if αἰών be derived from ἀεί 'always,' which I greatly doubt. The word never is used anywhere else in Scripture in the sense of endlessness (vulgarly called eternity). It always meant, both in Scripture and out, a period of time. Else how could it have a plural—how could you talk of *the* æons, and æons of æons, as the Scripture does? Nay, more, how talk of οὗτος ὁ αἰών, which the translators, with laudable inconsistency, have translated 'this world,' *i.e.* this present state of things, 'Age,' 'dispensation,' or epoch—αἰώνιος, therefore, means, and must mean, belonging to an epoch, or the epoch, and αἰώνιος κόλασις is the punishment allotted to that epoch. Always bear in mind, what is so plain to honest readers—that our Lord and the Apostles always speak of being in the end of an age or æon, not as ushering in a new one—as come to judge and punish the old world, and to create a new one out of its ruins, or rather, as the S. S. better expresses it, to burn up the chaff and keep the wheat, *i.e.* all the elements of food as seed for the new world.

"I think you may say that our Lord took the popular doctrine because He found it, and tried to correct and purify it, and put it on a really moral ground. You may quote the parable of Dives and Lazarus (which was the emancipation from the Tartarus theory) as the one instance in which our Lord professedly opens the secrets of the next world, that He there represents Dives as still Abraham's child, under no despair, not cut off from Abraham's sympathy, and under a direct moral training, of which you see the fruit. He is gradually weaned from the selfish desire of indulgence for himself, to love and care for his brethren. A divine step forward in his life, which of itself proves him not to be lost. The impossibility of Lazarus getting to him, or *vice versâ*, expresses plainly the great truth, that each being where he ought to be at that time, interchange of place (*i.e.* of spiritual state) is impossible. But it says nothing against Dives rising out of his torment, when he has learnt the lesson of it, and going where he ought to go. The common interpretation is merely arguing in a circle, assuming that there are but two states of the dead, 'Heaven' and 'Hell,' and then trying at once to interpret the parable by the assumption, and to prove the assumption from the parable. Next, you may say that the English *damnation*, like the Greek κατάκρισις, is perhaps κρίσις simple, simply means condemnation, and is (thank God) retained in that sense in various of our formularies, where I always read it, *e.g.* 'eateth to himself damnation,' with sincere pleasure, as protests in favour of the true and rational meaning of the word, against the modern and narrower meaning.

"You may say that Fire and Worms, whether physical or spiritual, must in all logical fairness be supposed to do what fire and worms really do, viz., destroy decayed and dead matter, and set free its elements to enter into new organisms; that, as they are beneficent and purifying agents in this life, they must be supposed such in the future life, and that the conception of fire as an engine of torture is an unnatural use of that agent, and not to be attributed to God without blasphemy, unless you suppose that the suffering (like all which He inflicts) is intended to teach man something which he cannot learn elsewhere.

"You may say that the catch, 'All sin deserves infinite punishment, because it is against an Infinite Being,' is a worthless amphiboly, using the word infinite in two utterly different senses, and being a mere play on sound. That it is directly contradicted by Scripture, especially by our Lord's own words, which declare that every man (not merely the wicked) shall receive the due reward of his deeds, that he who knew not his Lord's will and did it not, shall be beaten with few stripes, and so forth. That the words 'He shall not go out till he has paid the uttermost farthing,' evidently imply (unless spoken in cruel mockery) that he may go out then, and that it is scandalous for Protestants to derive from thence the opposite doctrine, while they call the Papists rogues for proving the perpetual virginity of the B. V. Mary from exactly the same use of ἕως.

"Finally, you may call on them (and how well you could do it!) to rejoice that there is a fire of God the Father, whose name is Love, burning for ever unquenchably, to destroy out of every man's heart, and out of the hearts of all nations, and off the physical and moral world, all which offends and makes a lie. That into that fire the Lord will surely cast all shams, lies, hypocrisies, tyrannies, pedantries, false doctrines, yea, and the men who love them too well to give them up, that the smoke of their βασανισμός (*i.e.* the torment which makes men confess the truth, for *that* is the real meaning of it; βασανισμός means the *touch*-stone by which gold was tested) may ascend perpetually, for a warning and a beacon to all nations. . . .

God grant that . . . we may have courage to let the fire and the worm do their work—to say to Christ, These too are Thine, and out of Thine infinite love they have come. Thou requirest truth in the inward parts, and I will thank Thee for any means, however bitter, which Thou usest to make me true. I want to be an honest man, and a right man! And, oh joy, *Thou* wantest me to be so also. Oh joy, that though I long cowardly to quench Thy fire,

I cannot do it. Purge us, therefore, O Lord, though it be with fire. Burn up the chaff of vanity and self-indulgence, of hasty prejudices, second-hand dogmas—husks which do not feed my soul, with which I cannot be content, of which I feel ashamed daily—and if there be any grains of wheat in me, any word, or thought, or power of action which may be of use as seed for my nation after me, gather it, O Lord, into Thy garner.

"Yes, . . . because I believe in a God of Absolute and Unbounded Love, therefore I believe in a Loving Anger of His,[1] which will and must devour and destroy all which is decayed, monstrous, abortive in His universe, till all enemies shall be put under His feet, to be pardoned, surely, if they confess themselves in the wrong, and open their eyes to the truth. And God shall be All in All.

"Those last are wide words. It is he who limits them, not I who accept them in their fulness, who denies the verbal inspiration of Scripture.

"C. K."

LETTER to ——, 1857.[2]

"DEAR SIR, or MADAM (for your signature is not sufficiently legible for me to determine which of the

---

[1] *Vide* Sermon on "The Wages of Sin" (*Water of Life and other Sermons*).

[2] This letter was written in answer to one from an unknown correspondent asking for Mr. Kingsley's views on endless torment, and beginning thus:—"Sir—Mr. B—— was my confessor. Dr. P—— is now. Nevertheless I read all your books, and yesterday, in the midst of *Two Years Ago*, I knelt down and said, 'At last, O God, I love Thee! for I know that Thou art good.'"—Vide *Letters and Memories*, Vol. II.

two you are)—When I read of worms and fire, I suppose that they either are worms and fire literally, or are some things which so resemble in their action worms and fire as to be best described by these terms metaphorically—to be, what is vulgarly called, a 'spiritual fire,' and 'spiritual worms.' Whether of the two they be, this at least is certain :—The office of worms in this world is to prevent, while they seem to accelerate, putrefaction, and thereby to prevent infectious epidemics; to devour decaying matter, and render it thereby innoxious; finally, to transmute it into new, living, and healthy organisms. The office of fire in this world is much the same, to devour dead matter, all but the ash or inorganic constituents, which are left as manure for some future crop. I know no other worms, no other fire, on earth than these beneficent ones. I expect none other elsewhere, unless every creature of God is not good, and to be received with thanksgiving. If they be a literal fire and worms, then they must be this or nothing. If a metaphorical fire and worms, an '*ignis immaterialis*,' such as the old fathers talked of, then they must be like this, or Scripture (and the Lord Himself) is using words at random, or in a deceptive sense.

"The use of fire for torture, an utterly unnatural and monstrous abuse of that element, sprang up among men of devilish and unnatural cruelty. It remained for a later age to adopt the belief of those Rabbis who crucified our Lord, that God would abuse the powers of fire (for ever!) for the same fiendish purposes for which they abused it for an hour or two, in the case of some shrieking and writhing victim.

"The torture of worms, Herodotus tells us, was tried now and then by old Persian despots. The mind of man has as yet so far recoiled from imputing so refined a barbarity to the Supreme Being, as to suppose in some confused inconsistent way, that the fire of course is fire; but the worm—they don't know about. A fire which cannot be quenched, a worm which cannot die, I see existing, whether they be those or not of which our Lord spoke. I consider them among the most blessed revelations of the Gospel. I fancy that I see them burning and devouring everywhere in the spiritual world, as their analogues do in the physical. I know that they have done so on me, and that their operation, though exquisitely painful, is most healthful. I see the world trying to quench and kill them; I know too well that I often do the same ineffectually. But in the comfort that the worm cannot die, and the fire cannot be quenched, I look calmly forward through endless ages, to my own future and the future of that world whereof it is written, 'He shall reign till he hath put all his enemies under his feet. The last enemy that shall be destroyed is death.' And again, 'Death and hell shall be cast into the lake of fire.'

"Of the parable of the sheep and goats, I have only to say, that our Lord speaks it expressly of Nations, and that neither you nor I are a nation; therefore the parable need give us no present selfish disquiet, though it may set us on reading Gibbon's *Decline and Fall*, as showing how our Lord's words came true fully and literally; set us thinking what a Nation means, and whether it be not better to help to save England than to try to deliver each 'his own life for a prey,' 'that this ruin may not lie upon our hand.' This would naturally set us on reading the Hebrew prophets, to whom, as to the rest of the Old Testament writers, the rabbinical Tartarus was unknown, and in due time we should come to that verse in Isaiah concerning the worm and the fire, which our Lord quotes in the Gospels, and to other words about the fire of God, and its effect on nations and individuals, from which we might rise up with more reverence than before for the letter of Holy Scripture, especially if, as churchmen, we held that the Old Testament was not contrary to the New. . . .

"Your obedient Servant,

"C. KINGSLEY."

LETTER to JOHN BULLAR, Esq.[1]

"*March* 12, 1856.

"Your letters . . . weigh me down with the thought of how little one knows—and after all how little man knows. . . . .

. . . . . .

"As for speculations as to what man's soul or unseen element is, and what happens to it when he dies—theories of Elysium and Tartarus, and of the future of this planet and its inhabitants—I leave them to those who see no miracles in every blade of grass, no unfathomable mysteries in every animalcule, and to whom Scripture is an easy book, of which they have mastered every word, by the convenient process of ignoring three-fourths of it. I don't complain of them; they are happier than I. If they saw more than they do, perhaps it would cripple them, dazzle, and terrify them. And it is a very great and priceless blessing to the country, that some sixteen thousand tolerably well-bred and necessarily respect-

---

[1] Vide *Letters and Memories*, Early Edition, Vol. I., of 1877, for whole letter.

able persons should be set up by the law, to tell people, in some confused way, yet truly, that doing wrong is infinitely harmful, and doing right is infinitely blessed and useful, and that God is (more or less, according to each man's scheme) a good God, and a living God, and a God who watches them, and will by no means clear the guilty, and will in some way have mercy on the penitent and reward the righteous doer; and that He has proved this by sending His Son to be made man, and die for men, though the reason of the latter fact, like the extent of the former one, they may not be able to speak of very rationally or coherently. If they be not scriptural, at least they make the Church, as she should be, a 'witness and keeper of Holy Writ,' and preserve it for generations happier than ours, who will find in it, I doubt not, treasures of which we never dreamed, even though they may cease to impute to Scripture the infallibility which it never claims, much more to deny its flat declarations for the sake of their own theories. You complain that the Church of England is fallen to a low ebb. She is no lower (I think her a great deal higher) than any other Christian denomination. She will be higher as long as she keeps her Articles, which bind men to *none* of the popular superstitions, but are so cautious, wide, and liberal, that I could almost believe them to have come down from heaven. But as soon as a generation of Bishops arises (either High or Low) who persist in demanding of candidates for ordination the popular creed, making those Articles mean that creed, and nothing else; then God help us; for the day of the Lord will be at hand, and will be revealed in flaming fire, not merely to give new light and a day-spring from on high to those who sit in darkness and the shadow of death, but to burn up out of sight, and off the universe, the chaff, hay, and stubble which men have built on the One Living Foundation, Christ—in that unquenchable fire, of which it is written that DEATH and HELL shall one day be cast into it also, to share the fate of all other unnatural and abominable things; and God's universe be—(what it must be some day, unless it be a failure, the imperfect work of an imperfect workman, and God is to be eternally baffled by evil)—very good. How that will happen I know not, neither care. But I know how it will *not* happen; not by God having, as some fancy, to destroy this planet as a failure and a blot, nor by the larger part of the human race passing endless time in irremediable torments. One such case ought to be enough to destroy the happiness of all the saved (unless they are grown suddenly cruel), and keep all heaven one everlasting agony of compassion. To believe that God should determine to torments endless one whom He could reform, is an insult to His love and justice, which I will die rather than utter. And it is an equal insult to His wisdom to say that He is too—— (what words shall I use without blasphemy?) to be unable to reform, convince, persuade, and soften the worst and stupidest heart—I mean even merely externally by actual argument, by reformatory discipline, however severe, which should prove to the man by sharp pangs that he was a fool, and that evil-doing would not pay; and by that winning love, returning good for evil, which, as we all know, is the most powerful of all to soften and convert: but much more by the most powerful influence of all, the direct transcendental working of God's Spirit on the man's spirit, which, I suppose, we are to believe in, unless we are Arminians.

"Till mankind have come to their senses on this point, I see but little hope for Christianity; and between me and the hearts of all good men, whom I long to embrace, that horrible dream yawns as a great gulf fixed. I cannot look them in the face without an effort, because I know that they hold a notion which is to me an immoral superstition, borrowed from the old heathens and rabbis (though our Tartarus is ten times as cruel and immoral as Virgil's), and of which no apostle seems to know anything whatever; and worse, because I know they would regard me with horror if they knew that I disbelieved it.

"Therefore, if you, like the rest, believe in Tartarus, and hold that our Lord came to promulgate that doctrine, and not (as His plain words seem to me to do) to correct those very notions in the rabbis which have descended to us from them, then let us not try to hold any more counsel together concerning the deep things of God. It will not be honest on either side, if both our theology and our anthropology differ by one enormous and all-important postulate. Let us talk of sanitary and social reform, and of birds and flowers, of the little pleasures of the sunshine and the spring, which are still allowed to the human race before it descends into endless flame, agony, and despair, while a few (and, perhaps, I among them) ascend to a heaven where I should be ashamed to be happy for one moment. Meanwhile, I shall cherish in secret the hope that the night is nigh past, that if not I, yet at least my children, will see a second European reformation—Tartarus follow its more foolish, but far less immoral and infernal child Purgatory, and the whole of Christendom leap up as men freed suddenly from the weight of a hideous nightmare to give thanks and glory to Him who descended into hell, and 'harrowed it,' as the glorious old words, now long forgotten, say, when He died for us and all mankind.

"Yours affectionately,

"C. KINGSLEY."

MS. LETTER to Mrs. ——.

"EVERSLEY RECTORY, *February* 2, 1860.

"Dear Madam—I fear seeming as not to sympathise enough with you; and yet I shrink from commonplace words of condolence, as almost insulting in the face of such an immeasurable woe.[1] I suppose that I had better turn myself at once to the doubt at which you have hinted, and answer, Believe your own heart; believe your mother's God-given instincts. Whatever is or is not the voice of God, *they* are. Believe, on the other hand, no man, or book, or angel out of heaven, who tells you that such as you have described to me are not safe— unless the devil, and not God, be the author of the universe; and answer to your preachers, if they dare doubt it, with Laertes—

> ' I tell thee, churlish priest,
> A ministering angel shall my sister be
> When thou liest howling.'

Believe me, madam, that the passages of Scripture

---

[1] The death, within a fortnight, of three young and lovely daughters, of whose salvation some religious friends of their mother's said, there could be no certainty, as they had not been consciously converted, and were therefore "unregenerate," and their virtues only "natural virtues."

which threaten punishment to the wicked, can only be made to include such persons as you describe by the most shameful twisting; that the argument which proves such to be wicked because their virtues are only 'natural virtues' (should they have been *un*natural then?) is nowhere to be found in Scripture, which *never* speaks of, or hints at, '*natural* goodness' as distinguished from the grace of God, but considers throughout, *all* goodness, wheresoever found, as God's gift.

"All goodness, and therefore your daughters' goodness, comes from God, and is the inspiration of the Holy Spirit of Christ and of God. But how inhuman to make that very truth a reason for denying their goodness, and for saying, 'All goodness comes from God's Spirit, and therefore theirs was no goodness, because they had not God's Spirit, being unregenerate.' Inhuman—because, instead of assuming their goodness as a proof that they are regenerate, it assumes, from a private system of these false teachers, that they are not regenerate—and immoral also, because, in order to suit that same system, it dares to say that goodness is not goodness, sapping thereby the very sense of right and wrong in the human heart, and leaving no standard of virtue at all. No wonder that many a one who has begun by despising what he calls 'natural virtues,' has ended (as I have seen) by becoming the slave of most *un*natural vices.

"Madam, when I hear such doctrine as that which you too truly call the 'general religious doctrine' propounded in sermons, which fall harmless from their sheer stupidity, I can afford to smile, and wait for better times; but when I find that doctrine torturing a living human heart (as it must when it is faced honestly), and that heart a mother's, then what humanity and chivalry there may be in me is roused to bitter indignation; and I bid you, in spite of all preachers and systems, listen to God's voice in your heart, and be not afraid of their terror, neither be troubled, but sanctify the Lord God in your heart. Sanctify Him—believe Him to be just and good, and take refuge with Him from doctrines which would make Him unjust and cruel beyond all words. Take refuge in your Bible, and when men tell you, and truly, that the greatest proof of the Bible's divineness is that it meets the needs of the human heart, take them at their word, and answer, 'Then I will not believe that as soon as I go to my Bible in real need, and real agony, it answers me with doctrines which outrage my human heart, outrage my sense of justice and mercy, and insult my sorrow by heaping on it fresh horror.'

"And remember this, madam, that though this may be the teaching of the popular religious world, yet it is not the teaching of God's Church. God's Church tells you that your daughters are regenerate in baptism, partakers of God's Holy Spirit, members of Christ, children of God, and inheritors of the kingdom of heaven. Believe that—the doctrine of apostles, of prophets, of saints and martyrs, of the Church of England; and leave the other doctrine, with its inhuman contradictions and doubts, to those who, having subscribed to our Liturgy and Articles, deny from the pulpit the very doctrines which they have sworn that they believe.

"Leave them to face the woes pronounced against those who make the heart of the righteous sad, whom God hath not made sad, while they comfort the wicked, if he will only cant, by promising him life;— against those who call evil good, and good evil;

against those who cause Christ's little ones to stumble; against those who are themselves stumbling, in their blindness, on the very edge of the unpardonable sin against the Holy Ghost, by saying of the Christlike (because they do not happen—any more than Christ did—to belong to the Pharisees), 'He hath a devil.'

"I write strongly, madam, but deliberately. I think I may bring comfort to you by telling you to defy and cast out these thoughts, and those who preach them, and cast yourself upon God, whose name is Love, and His essence Justice, and on that Church of God which tells you that your children are the children of God, and their good deeds and tempers the working of the Spirit of God. Believe that, and you will find a strength in that faith which will, I trust, bear you up under a trial which I can only contemplate with a horror which finds no words to express itself.

"God bless you and keep you, my dear madam.

"Your faithful Servant,

"C. Kingsley."

For the Private Consideration of the Committee for the Defence of the Athanasian Creed.[1]

"This seems to me the time for sound Churchmen to use a fresh weapon in defence of the Athanasian Creed, by bringing forward a somewhat neglected

---

[1] Mr. Kingsley's name was placed on the Committee for the Defence of the Athanasian Creed; but being unable to attend one of the meetings, he sent this letter.—Vide *Letters and Memories*, Early Edition, Vol. II.

Catholic doctrine—that of the intermediate state, or states. Thus, too, I may say in passing, the Church would be shown to be on this—as on other points—more and not less liberal than her dissenting opponents.

"The Athanasian Creed is now construed by the people in the light of Puritan Eschatology—*i.e.* of the doctrine which the Puritans (as far as I know) introduced first, namely, that the fate of every man is irrevocably fixed at the moment of death.

"I need not tell you that this is not the Catholic doctrine; that the Church has held, from a very early age, the belief in an intermediate state. That belief was distorted and abused, in later times, as the Romish doctrine of Purgatory. But the denunciation of that doctrine in the Thirty-nine Articles (as Dr. Newman pointed out, if I recollect rightly, in Tract 90) does not denounce any primitive doctrine of Purgatory, nay, rather allows it, by the defining adjective 'Romish.' That this Puritan Eschatology is no part of the Creed of the Church of England is proved by her final rejection of the Article affirming endless punishment.

"It is as well here to say, that I do not *deny* endless punishment. On the contrary, I believe it possible for me and other Christian men, by loss of God's grace, to commit acts of $\dot{a}\tau a\sigma\theta a\lambda\acute{\iota}a$—sins against light and knowledge, which would plunge us into endless abysses of probably increasing and endless punishment.

"But I say that to predicate endless punishment, from the moment of death of those who either sin, or misbelieve, not of $\dot{a}\tau a\sigma\theta a\lambda\acute{\iota}a$, but of weakness or invincible ignorance, is not required by the Church of England, nor (as far as I am aware) by the

Churches of Rome or of Greece; and that the doctrine of an intermediate state has been in all Christian ages and lands (save where Puritan influences have prevailed) the refuge of the sense of justice and pity in man from so terrible a doctrine.

"Now, it is plain again that men have no right to read the Athanasian Creed in this Puritan sense. In whatsoever age it was composed, it was composed by one who believed in the intermediate state; and there is nothing in its language to hint that he held that there was no hope in that state for the unorthodox whom he denounced; nothing to hint that he held, with the old Crusaders, that an infidel went straight to hell. So guardedly vague are the expressions of the Creed as to 'perishing everlastingly,' and 'everlasting salvation,' that it might be believed and used honestly by one who did not hold the 'necessary immortality of the soul,' and therefore thought the final annihilation of the wicked possible.

"The Creed says, and truly, that the knowledge of God, and it alone, is everlasting life. It does not say that that knowledge may not be vouchsafed hereafter to those who have sought honestly for it in this life, but through unfortunate circumstances, or invincible ignorance, have failed to find it. Provided the search be honestly continued in the unknown realms beyond the grave, the Athanasian Creed does not deny that the seeker, it may be after heavy pains and long wanderings, shall not at last discover his Saviour and his God, and discover that for Him he had been yearning though he knew it not.

"It is almost needless for me to point out how such an interpretation of the Athanasian Creed would relieve the consciences of thousands, without (it seems to me) forfeiting our strict honesty, or our claim to

Catholic orthodoxy—how it would make the Creed tolerable to thousands to whom (under its Puritan misrepresentation) it is now intolerable; and would render unnecessary that alteration of the so-called 'damnatory clauses,' to which I have consented with much unwillingness, and only as a concession to the invincible ignorance of modern Puritanism.

"I have reason to believe that the English mind (and possibly the Scotch) is specially ripe just now for receiving once more this great Catholic doctrine of the intermediate state, and that by preaching it with all prudence, as well as with all manfulness, we should cut the ground from under our so-called 'Liberal' adversaries' feet. I say—with all prudence. For it is plain that unguarded latitude of expression might easily awaken a cry that we were going to introduce 'the Romish doctrine of Purgatory,' and to proceed to 'pardons' and 'masses for the dead.' But that if we keep cautiously within the limits permitted by truly Catholic antiquity, we shall set in motion a mighty engine for the Church's help in her need, I, as a student of public opinion, have no doubt whatsoever. While I fear, on the other hand, that unless we take the course I have pointed out, we shall lose, to our extreme injury, not only on the so-called 'damnatory clauses,' but (for all practical purposes) the Creed itself.

"CHARLES KINGSLEY.

"*November* 1872."

THE END

www.ingramcontent.com/pod-product-compliance
Lightning Source LLC
Chambersburg PA
CBHW021942160426
43195CB00011B/1190